LOVE VEGAN

The Essential Mexican Cookbook for Vegans

Zoe Hazan

HIGH CEDAR PRESS

LOVE VEGAN

The Essential Mexican Cookbook for Vegans

High Cedar Press

Copyright © 2017

Kindle Edition

Published by High Cedar Press

Illustrations Copyright © 2017

DISCLAIMER

TThe full contents of 'Love Vegan', including text, comments, graphics, images, and other content are for informational purposes only. The information is not intended to diagnose, treat, cure or prevent any illnesses or diseases. Always consult you physician before changing dietary habits.

'Love Vegan' does not provide specific information or advice regarding food intolerance or allergies. It is the responsibility of the reader to ensure any diagnosed or potential food intolerances are identified and excluded from the recipes.

The author and publisher make no guarantee as to the availability of ingredients mentioned in this book. Many ingredients vary in size and texture and these differences may affect the outcome of some recipes. The author has tried to make the recipes as accurate and workable as possible, however, cannot be responsible for any recipe not working.

Every effort has been made to prepare this material to ensure it's accuracy, however, the author nor publisher will be held responsible if there is information deemed as inaccurate.

CONTENTS

• •

MAINS

SIDES

Kale & Spinach Salad with Creamy Avocado Dressing	63
7 Layer Mexican Dip	65
Vegan Elote (Mexican Street Corn)	66

EXTRAS

Roasted Garlic Mashed Potatoes	69
Homemade Taco Sauce	71
Vegan Sour Cream	73
Chimichurri Sauce	74
Restaurant Style Salsa	75
Salsa Verde	76
Vegan Mexican Cheese	77

DESERTS

Horchata (Sweet Mexican Rice Milk)	80
Mexican Hot Chocolate	81
Crispy Mexican Churros	82
Pineapple & Apple Empanadas	84
Chili Chocolate Avocado Mousse	86
Mayan Spiced Chocolate Pudding	87
Buñuelos (Cinnamon-Sugar Crisps)	89

INTRODUCTION

From Fully Loaded Nachos and Wedges with Vegan Nacho Cheese to Sweet Mexican Rice Milk and Crispy Mexican Churros, this cookbook celebrates the flavors of Mexico and shows you how easy it is to prepare authentic and delicious vegan dishes in your very own kitchen - on even the busiest of weeknights.

Mexican food has become increasingly popular throughout the Western world where you will see Mexican restaurants popping up on your local high street and ready made Mexican meals on the supermarket shelves. Traditional Mexican cuisine is a fusion of the ancient Aztec and Mayan Indians with ingredients and cooking techniques that originated from all over the world including Spanish and Indian influences.

The basic staples of this cuisine come in the form of simple, easy to source, natural ingredients such as corn, pulses, and rice - making it very easy to adapt Mexican recipes to the vegan diet.

Our philosophy is to bring an authentic Mexican street food flavor to vegans all over the world and to enable you to enjoy vegan versions of your favorite meals such as Fajitas, Burritos and Chili, along with delicious desserts including Churros and Chili Chocolate Avocado Mousse.

The recipes have been carefully tried, tested and refined to retain an authentic taste and texture, yet use simple and straight-forward ingredients found in your local supermarket. The emphasis is on cooking traditional, authentically flavored dishes for even the most inexperienced of cooks, making your life simpler and your meal preparation easier.

Whether you are a vegan, vegetarian or meat-eater looking to reduce the amount of animal produce in your diet, the 'Love Vegan' series of cookbooks will inspire you to cook delicious authentically flavored Mexican vegan dishes on even the busiest of weeknights.

VEGANISM FOR BEGINNERS

Did you know the average meat-eater consumes three times the amount of protein daily than their bodies need? As people are becoming more aware of the dangers of consuming large quantities of meat-based produce the movement towards a plant based diet grows in popularity.

Vegans choose to consume no animal products for either ethical or dietary reasons and this book strives to ensure that vegan food is never bland or boring. 'Love Vegan' proves that fresh and flavorsome food is simple and easy to make in your very own kitchen.

Whether you want to go completely vegan, or simply add vegan food to your diet to give your body a healthy boost, the 'Love Vegan' cookbook series will give you many mouth-watering meals to tantalise your taste buds and make the transition to a meat-free life a little easier.

THE FLAVORS OF MEXICO

Let's take a look at some of the flavors and staple ingredients from around the country and see how easy it is to adapt them to the vegan diet, while still retaining the taste, texture and delicious Mexican flavor.

Avocado: These creamy and buttery fruits are the perfect compliment to spicy Mexican dishes. They are most commonly used in guacamole but can be used to incorporate a delicious creamy element to any dish.

Pulses: Beans are also known as Frijoles in Mexico, and are a very common ingredient found in a lot of Mexican dishes. The most used pulses in Mexican cuisine are black and pinto beans, which lend their flavor and texture to refried beans - a popular dish made by soaking dried beans, adding spices, and then mashing and frying them.

Cheeses: 'Love Vegan' has some mouth-watering vegan cheese recipes to die for! Whether you are looking for a touch of cheesy flavor to sprinkle on a burrito, or you wish to drizzle some queso on your loaded nachos, this book has some deliciously creamy and flavorsome vegan cheese substitutes that can rival any dairy based version!

Chilies: The most dominant flavor within Mexican food, and most likely what comes to mind when you think of Mexican flavoring. There are many different types that are commonly used including smoked, dried, fresh or picked. Some of the most popular varieties include ancho chilies (mild and sweet), habanero (extremely hot!), jalapeno (the most common) and pasilla (mild to medium heat).

Limes: Lime is widely used throughout Mexican cooking in recipes such as salsa, guacamole, and marinades for a burst of zesty fresh flavor.

Tortillas: These soft pancake-like flatbreads are eaten with most Mexican dishes, They are much healthier and contain less calories than other shades such as bread or pasta.

Coriander: Coriander or cilantro is the most commonly used fresh herb in Mexican cooking. It is slightly sweet with a hint of lemon that compliments the flavors of Mexican cooking perfectly.

Tomatoes: Many Mexican dishes use chopped tomatoes as the base for the sauce and then add lots of vibrant flavors. Dishes such as salsa, burritos, and stews use tomatoes as the main ingredient.

MEXICAN PANTRY STAPLES

Mexican dishes are very easy to make as they do not usually feature a lot of ingredients. To make your life easier and to ensure your kitchen is equipt with staple items most commonly used in Mexican cooking it is advisable that you have a well-stocked pantry to avoid a last minute trip to the supermarket after a long day at work.

The list below is a variety of simple ingredients that you should keep in your cupboards so that you are ready to whip up a delicious authentic Mexican dish at any time.

- Tinned pulses (black, pinto, butter and kidney beans)
- Tinned tomatoes
- Fresh Garlic
- Fresh Coriander
- Dried Oregano
- Cumin Powder
- Chilis - fresh, dried and powdered
- Vegetable Stock
- Quinoa
- Brown Rice
- Nutritional Yeast (to mimic a 'cheesy' flavor)
- Tofu
- Fresh and Frozen Vegetables (including corn)
- Tortilla wraps (can be frozen)

EATING FOR OPTIMAL HEALTH

'To keep the body in good health is a duty...otherwise we shall not be able to keep our mind strong and clear' - Buddha

There is a growing movement across the Western world where people are becoming more aware of what they are eating and the health and nutritional benefits of food. Healthy eating, along with eliminating or reducing meat intake has become more of a lifestyle decision as opposed to a fad diet.

Veganism is not a fad diet that is only supposed to last for a certain duration. It is a way of life that goes much deeper than just eating plant based food. People choose a vegan diet for many reasons – sometimes it is because they don't want to buy meat from unethical meat farms that treat their animals badly. Other times it is due to a need to simplify their diet and to bring their bodies to optimum health.

Vegan foods offer your body high-quality nutrition. The foods are easily digested and are quickly assimilated into your system, thus providing you with an abundance of energy, enough to sustain you for a long period of time.

Beans and legumes are an excellent source of energy, for example, the Black Bean Flautas featured in this book is a lunch option that will keep you feeling full of energy for the entire afternoon. You won't have that lethargic feeling that your body gets when the processed and starchy foods you have consumed leave your body sluggish and tired, and all your energy has been taken up trying to digest the heavy carbohydrates in your stomach.

Whether you are a vegan, vegetarian or meat-eater trying to reduce the amount of meat you consume, the 'Love Vegan' cookbook series is here to make your life easier, healthier and most certainly tastier!

One of the first assumptions made with regards to the vegan lifestyle is that a plant based diet cannot possibly provide you with enough nutrients, vitamins, and mineral to help sustain a healthy and balanced life. This assumption is based around the idea that protein, calcium, iron and other important nutrients are only available by consuming animal produce, however, this could not be further from the truth.

Have a look below at the varied ingredients vegans can consume in order to live a healthy and balanced life:

PROTEIN

Protein is always the first thing anyone asks a vegan about because of the misconception that without meat it is difficult to source enough protein.

Nuts, legumes, and pulses are a fantastic source of protein- and luckily for vegans Mexican food is filled with them! You could try the refried beans or the Spicy Black Bean Soup to help you get the recommended daily intake of protein.

Quinoa is also a great source of protein with 1 cup providing you with around 8g of your daily needs - why not try a serving of the Mexican Quinoa.

A typical man needs approx. 56g grams of protein per day and a woman requires 46g. Keep in mind that this figure will change according to each individual's body weight and lifestyle. Reaching your recommended daily amount of protein on a plant based diet really isn't as difficult as many people assume and should not be too much of a challenge.

FATS

For fats, opt for healthy fats found in olives, avocados, coconuts (coconut oil, dairy-free milk, and cream), seeds and nuts. All of these now have oils made out of them that can be found on your supermarket shelves and are a great alternative to olive oil for cooking.

CARBOHYDRATES

When choosing carbohydrates, try to choose complex carbohydrates such as whole grains and stay away from refined grains, choosing brown rice over white.

Opt for whole wheat buns for your burgers or even leave the bun out and substitute it with two big, juicy, portobello mushrooms for a delicious alternative. The recipe for Sweet Potato Burger with Avocado can seriously rival any meat burger and satisfy meat cravings.

VITAMINS

When it comes to vitamins, load up on fresh fruits and vegetables which are jam packed with nutrients, vitamins, fibre and antioxidants.

Frozen berries are a great source of vitamin C and antioxidants, and make a mouthwatering vegan dessert or snack on a hot summer's day, as well as being so very tasty when used in a smoothie.

Eating vegan food is about integrating a wide variety of colorful produce into your diet, and in that way, you cover all your nutritional needs and well as satisfying your taste buds.

LOVE VEGAN

Most of us don't want to spend an hour in the kitchen preparing dinner after a long hard all day, however, the 'Love Vegan' Cookbook series proves that you can stay healthy and enjoy quick and easy to cook Mexican cuisine on even the busiest of weeknights. The best part is that most recipes will take less than half an hour to prepare.

The type of Mexican cuisine you would find in restaurants relies heavily on meat, cheese, and dishes that are high in carbs. Finding vegan cheese can be a challenge and is likely to have chemicals and preservatives in it, but now you can make your own within this recipe book. It is easy and you can flavor it with whatever spice you want.

Mexican food need not be complicated to make. Our featured recipes contain basic, straightforward, wholesome and natural ingredients that you can easily find in your local supermarket or farmer's market. The aim of this book and the 'Love Vegan' series is to make eating vegan food a pleasure as well as filling your body with nourishing food that is quick to prepare.

There is no better way to mark special occasions than with tasty homemade food. From birthdays, Thanksgiving or Christmas to a lazy family Sunday BBQ - we have the perfect vegan option for every occasion. Put in your tender loving flair and you will create a mouthwatering array of recipes that will leave you feeling like a professional chef.

SUMMARY

We love Mexican food because its dishes are spicy, colorful, and full of flavor.

This cookbook is focused on basic, natural and wholesome ingredients, and when cooked in the right way and perfectly flavored you can create beautiful, authentic and mouth-watering vegan dishes, regardless of your cooking ability.

Whether you are a long term follower of the vegan lifestyle, a beginner in need of an easy way to get started or a meat-eater looking to incorporate a meat-free Monday into your week, this book will give you some deliciously authentic recipes for any occasion.

So get ready for some exciting and easy to cook vegan meals that will open up a whole new world for you.

MAINS

TEMPEH TEQUILA TACO SLIDERS

These wonderfully little taco sliders are a welcoming alternative to traditional tacos. These crowd-pleasing tacos make an impressive appetizer for a get-together, and are also perfect for game day!

Preparation Time
20 minutes
(+ overnight for
cashews to soak)

Total Time
50 minutes

Makes
4 servings / 8 sliders

INGREDIENTS

FOR THE SLIDERS:

8oz / 225g soy tempeh
¼ cup tequila
2 tbsp maple syrup, divided
2 tbsp lime juice
1 tbsp canola or vegetable oil
½ medium white onion, finely chopped
2 cloves garlic, finely chopped
1 red bell pepper, thinly sliced
½ tsp salt
½ tsp black pepper
1 tsp dried oregano
½ tsp ground cumin
¼ tsp coriander powder
¼ tsp cayenne pepper

FOR THE CASHEW SOUR CREAM:

¼ cup cashew nuts (soaked overnight)
¼ tsp apple cider vinegar
¼ tsp lemon juice
Pinch of salt

8 slider buns or mini corn tortillas
¼ head iceberg lettuce, thinly sliced
1 large avocado, chopped
Handful of cilantro, roughly chopped

DIRECTIONS

Slice tempeh into 8 squares. Mix together ¼ cup of tequila,

maple syrup, and lime juice then add the tempeh, coating each slice thoroughly with the liquid. Set aside to marinade while you move onto the next steps.

Drain and rinse the cashew nuts then place them in a blender along with the water, apple cider vinegar, lemon juice, and salt and blend until smooth, scraping down the sides as you go along. Transfer to a bowl then chill in the fridge until you are ready to serve.

Heat a skillet with oil and sauté onions for 3-4 minutes until soft. Add the garlic, stirring for a minute then the red pepper, seasoning and all of the spices. Cook for 8-10 minutes until the pepper has softened. Add a dash of water if the mixture gets a little dry.

While the peppers are softening you can cook the tempeh by either placing it in a steamer for 5-7 minutes or heat up a clean skillet with a little oil and fry it over medium-high heat for 8 minutes (4 minutes on each side). Be sure to keep the marinade.

Add the tempeh to the pepper mixture along with the marinade and cook for 10 minutes until everything has heated thoroughly.

To make the sliders add 1/8th of the tempeh mixture to each slider bun or tortilla. Top with lettuce, a dollop of cashew sour cream, a few chunks of avocado and garnish with cilantro.

SMOKY CHILI WEDGES WITH NACHO CHEESE SAUCE

Crisp and fluffy Mexican spiced wedges with creamy melted nacho cheese, and best of all this dish is 100% vegan! The cheese sauce is so versatile you can use it with other recipes.

Preparation Time	**Total Time**	**Makes**
15 minutes	50 minutes	4 servings

INGREDIENTS

FOR THE POTATO WEDGES:

3 large white potatoes, unpeeled & cut into wedges
2 tsp olive oil
2 tsp ground cumin
½ tsp chili powder
1 tsp ground coriander
1 tsp garlic powder
1 ½ tsp smoked paprika
½ - 1 tsp cayenne pepper
1 tsp dried oregano
½ tsp smoked salt or coarse salt
½ tsp freshly ground black pepper
2 tbsp fresh cilantro, chopped

FOR THE NACHO CHEESE SAUCE:

2 medium potatoes, peeled & chopped
3 large carrots, peeled & chopped
½ cup nutritional yeast
⅓ cup olive oil
⅓ cup water
1 tbsp freshly squeezed lemon juice
1½ tsp coarse salt
1-2 jalapenos, finely chopped (optional)

DIRECTIONS

TO MAKE THE POTATO WEDGES:

Preheat the oven to 350° / 180°. Grease a baking tray with a little olive oil.

Place the potato wedges in large mixing bowl and add the oil, cumin, chili powder, coriander, garlic, paprika, cayenne, dried oregano, and seasoning. Mix well until fully combined and each potato wedge is coated with the flavoring.

Transfer the wedges to the greased baking tray and move them around so that they are in a single layer. This will enable them to get really crispy. If you find there are too many to fit on your baking tray you may need to use two.

Bake the wedges for 35-40 minutes, flipping them over once halfway through cooking.

While the wedges are baking you can prepare the cheese sauce.

TO MAKE THE NACHO CHEESE SAUCE:

Place potatoes and carrots in a steamer and steam until soft and tender. If you do not have a steamer you can boil the vegetables using the following method: Place potatoes, carrots and ½ tsp salt in a saucepan and fill with just enough water to cover. Bring to a boil and cook for 5-7 minutes until tender when pierced with a fork.

Once the vegetables have cooked add to a food processor and blend along with nutritional yeast, olive oil, water, lemon juice, and salt until smooth and creamy.

Remove from the blender and stir in chopped jalapenos.

Remove wedges from the oven and transfer to a serving plate. Garnish with chopped cilantro and serve with the nacho cheese. You can either drizzle the cheese on top or serve it on the side as a dip.

.

FULLY LOADED NACHOS

There are three different recipes that you will need to prepare beforehand - cheese sauce, salsa, and chili, but believe us when we say it will be worth your time! You can serve this dish without any one of these elements if you wish to reduce the preparation time, however, it is highly recommended to include all three!

Preparation Time	**Total Time**	**Makes**
10 minutes	15 minutes *	2-3 as a main

*(+ additional time to make the cheese sauce, salsa, and chili which are all recipes within this cookbook)

INGREDIENTS

1 large bag tortilla chips
2 cup Nacho Cheese Sauce
1 cup Mexican Salsa
2 cups Quinoa Chili
1 can black beans
1 large tomato, chopped
¾ cup corn
4-5 scallions chopped
1 avocado, peeled, pitted and chopped
2-3 jalapenos, finely chopped
¼ cup fresh cilantro, roughly chopped
½ cup sliced black olives

DIRECTIONS

Layer ¹/₃ of the tortilla chips at the bottom of a large serving bowl then dollop with ¹/₃ of the chili and ¹/₃ of the salsa. Drizzle with a $^1/_3$ of the cheese sauce, then sprinkle with half of the black beans.

Layer with another $^1/_3$ of the chips and dollop with a $^1/_3$ of the chili and a $^1/_3$ of the salsa. Drizzle with a $^1/_3$ of the cheese sauce, then sprinkle with remaining half of black beans.

Layer with remaining chips, chili and salsa. Drizzle with the remaining cheese sauce.

Top with the salsa, tomatoes, corn, scallions, olives, jalapeños, avocado, and cilantro. Serve immediately.

The nachos will keep in an airtight container in the fridge and will last 3-5 days.

BLACK BEAN FLAUTAS

A flauta is a traditional Mexican dish consisting of a rolled up tortilla, which has been stuffed with a choice of filling and then fried to create a golden crispy exterior. These authentically flavored flautas are perfect as a main dish with rice or as an appetiser.

Preparation Time
10 minutes
(+ 15 minutes
for the sauce to
marinate)

Total Time
30 minutes

Makes
16 flautas / Serves
3-4

INGREDIENTS

½ cup red onion, finely chopped
¼ cup fresh cilantro leaves, chopped
1 large lime, freshly juiced
1 garlic clove, peeled and finely chopped
1 large lime, cut into wedges
2 cups refried beans

16 white corn tortillas, warmed
Vegetable or canola oil for frying
¼ head chopped lettuce
1 tomato, chopped

Toothpicks to hold flautas together while cooking

DIRECTIONS

In a small bowl combine red onion, cilantro, lime, and garlic and set aside for 10-15 minutes to marinate.

Heat ¼ inch of oil in a frying pan over medium heat.

Lay warmed tortilla out on a clean surface or chopping board and spread 1 heaped tablespoon of refried beans and ½ tablespoon of cilantro-lime mixture evenly over one side of the tortilla. Starting from the filling side, tightly roll each tortilla then secure it with a toothpick so it doesn't come undone while cooking. It is advised to roll around 3-4 at a time, fry these, and roll 4 more while each batch is cooking.

Fry the batch of flautas, seam side down for 4-5 minutes, gently flipping over once halfway through frying using a pair of tongs. Once they are golden brown and crisp on all sides remove the flautas using the tongs and transfer to a paper towel lined plate.

Continue with remaining tortilla wraps, and remove the toothpick once they have cooled down a little and are ready to serve.

Serve immediately while hot and crispy with lettuce, tomato and a dipping sauce of your choice. Sour Cream or Chimichurri works well.

CHILES RELLENOS (CHEESE STUFFED CHILIES)

These Mexican-style battered and fried chiles are crispy, spicy and have melted vegan cashew cheese stuffed into the middle. These truly are mouth-wateringly delicious!

Preparation Time
15 minutes
(+ 4 hours to soak cashews)

Total Time
40 minutes

Makes
4 Rellenos

INGREDIENTS

4 large poblano or hatch peppers, roasted, peeled

FOR THE CHEESE

1 cup raw cashews (soaked for a minimum of 4 hours)
1 clove of garlic, roughly chopped
1 tsp salt
¼ tsp garlic powder
1 heaped tbsp nutritional yeast
1 tsp tapioca flour or cornstarch

FOR THE TOMATO SAUCE

½ tbsp olive oil
½ onion, finely chopped
4 large tomatoes
2 cloves garlic, finely chopped
¼ tsp cumin powder
¼ tsp cayenne pepper
¼ tsp salt
⅛ tsp sugar

2 -3 cups canola or vegetable oil

FOR THE BATTER

1 cup all purpose flour, sieved
1 cup cornstarch
1 tsp salt
1 tsp cumin powder
½ tsp baking powder
1 ½ cups cold carbonated water

1 cup hot water

DIRECTIONS

Preheat the oven to 350°. Line a baking tray with parchment paper.

Roast the peppers for around 15-20 minutes, turning over twice, until the skin starts to blister on all sides. Remove from the oven and set aside. Once they are cool enough to touch remove the blackened skin from the chiles then slice them vertically from the stem to the top. Set aside.

While the chiles are cooling you can move onto the cheese. Drain and rinse the cashew nuts. Place all cheese ingredients in a high-speed blender or food processor and blend until completely smooth. Pour the cheese sauce into a heavy bottomed saucepan and whisk constantly over medium-low heat until it becomes thick and gooey. Set aside while you make the tomato sauce.

Place all tomato sauce ingredients in a saucepan and cook over medium heat until the onions have softened and the tomatoes have broken down, around 5-6 minutes. Allow to cool for a moment or two then carefully transfer into a food processor and blitz until completely smooth.

Heat the oil to around 350°.

Fill the chiles by laying them, sliced side up, and gently open them up. Fill each chile with the cheese sauce and close the chiles over the filling - you can use a toothpick to secure them if you prefer.

To make the batter whisk flour, cornstarch, salt, cumin, and baking powder until well combined then mix in carbonated water.

Dip each chili into the batter, letting any excess batter drip off and gently lower into the hot oil. Fry until golden, around 4 minutes on each side. Do not overcrowd the pan as this will lower the temperature of the oil and prevent the Rellenos from becoming crispy.

Remove from the oil and transfer to a paper towel lined plate. Serve the Rellenos immediately on top of the tomato sauce.

POZOLE (TRADITIONAL MEXICAN STEW)

Pozole is a traditional soup or stew from Mexico. This beloved recipe is as authentic as you can get and is commonly served at special occasions. The recipe requires an ingredient called hominy which are puffy and chewy kernels of corn that have a deep nutty flavor. If you are unable to source hominy you can substitute it for corn kernels, however, the essence of this soup lies within the use of the hominy.

Preparation Time
20 minutes

Total Time
20 minutes

Makes
4 servings

INGREDIENTS

4 medium dried ancho chiles, stemmed
1 tbsp olive oil
1 medium onion, chopped
3 garlic cloves, peeled
1 tsp dried oregano
1 tsp apple cider vinegar
½ tsp sugar
1 heaped tsp cumin
12oz / 340g firm tofu
4 cups vegetable stock
2 cups water

1 tsp salt
1 can (29oz / 820g) hominy, drained and rinsed (also labeled pozole or monet blanco)
1 can (14oz / 400g) kidney beans
2 cups cabbage, shredded
1 cup sliced radishes
¼ lime

DIRECTIONS

Place dried chiles in a bowl and top with enough hot water to fully submerge them. Leave them to soften for 20 minutes.

Remove tofu from packaging and press between two towels to remove excess water. You can use something weighted, such as a large saucepan or a heavy chopping board and place this on top of the tofu to squeeze out as much moisture as possible for a minimum of 10 minutes. This process will allow the tofu to absorb much more flavor. After 10 minutes chop tofu into small cubes.

While the chiles are soaking and the tofu is being pressed heat oil in a large pot and sauté onions for 10 minutes, stirring frequently to prevent them from burning. Add the tofu and fry for 10 minutes until it has slightly browned on all sides.

Once the chiles have soaked place then in a food processor or high-speed blender along with 3 tbsp of the soaking water, garlic, oregano, apple cider vinegar, sugar, and cumin and blitz until you have a smooth paste. Add 1 tsp or more soaking water if the paste is too dry. Scrape down the sides of the blender as you go along to ensure all ingredients are fully combined.

Pour the vegetable stock, water, and salt into the onion-tofu mixture and scrape in the chili paste along with the hominy and kidney beans.

Bring to a boil then reduce to a low simmer and cook for 15-20 minutes over medium heat.

Serve with cabbage, radish, and a squeeze of lime juice.

This is a great make ahead dish as the stew will keep for up to 4 days in the fridge and you will find the flavor will enhance the longer you keep it.

THREE-BEAN QUINOA CHILI

This super healthy vegan, protein-packed chili is the perfect bowl of comfort food that is loaded with fresh pulses and quinoa, and packed full of spicy Mexican flavor.

Preparation Time
10 minutes

Total Time
40 minutes

Makes
6 servings

INGREDIENTS

1 tbsp olive oil
1 large onion, finely chopped
4 garlic cloves, minced
1-2 fresh chilies, finely chopped
2 (2 x 15oz / 420g) cans chopped tomatoes
1 (2 x 15oz / 420g) can tomato sauce
1 ½ cups vegetable stock
1 tbsp chili powder
1 tbsp cayenne pepper
1 tbsp cumin
1 tbsp paprika
1 tsp dried oregano
1 tsp ground coriander
1 tsp white sugar

1 tsp coarse salt
¾ tsp freshly ground pepper
¾ cups uncooked quinoa
1 ½ cups vegetable stock
1 (15oz / 420g) can kidney beans
1 (15oz / 420g) can black beans
1 (15oz / 420g) can pinto beans
1 ½ cups corn, fresh or frozen
½ cup cilantro leaves, chopped
Juice of 1 lime, freshly squeezed

DIRECTIONS

In a large saucepan heat olive oil, then add chopped onions and saute for 3-4 minutes until soft. Add garlic and fresh chili and cook for a minute.

Add the chili, cayenne, cumin, paprika, oregano, coriander

powder, sugar, salt and pepper, and stir for 30 seconds until fragrant.

Pour in the chopped tomatoes, tomato sauce, vegetable stock and dry quinoa. Bring to a boil then reduce to a low simmer. Cover and cook over low heat for 20 minutes.

Uncover, add the drained and rinsed beans, corn, cilantro leaves and lime juice, and cook uncovered for 15-20 minutes until the sauce has reduced and thickened.

.

SPICY SWEET POTATO BURGERS WITH SMASHED AVOCADO

TThese are such versatile burgers that they can be eaten inside a bun or alone with a side salad. The beans help the burger hold together to create a firm, flavorful and filling patty.

Preparation Time
10 minutes

Total Time
1 hour 10 minutes
(including cooking
time for sweet
potato)

Makes
8 patties / Serves 4
people

INGREDIENTS

1 large sweet potato, peeled
15oz / 420g can of white beans, drained and rinsed
½ cup white onion, chopped
2-3 tbsp tahini
1 tsp apple cider vinegar
1 tsp garlic powder
1 ½ tsp cajun spice or cayenne pepper
½ tsp coarse salt
½ tsp freshly ground black pepper

⅓ cup all-purpose flour (or oat / almond flour)
1 large avocado, peeled, sliced
½ lime, juiced
¼ tsp chili flakes

FOR THE TOPPINGS:

1 large tomato, sliced
¼ head lettuce, chopped

8 burger buns (optional)

DIRECTIONS

IPreheat the oven to 400° / 200° and grease a baking tray lightly with oil. Bake the sweet potato for around 45 minutes, or until the inside of soft and tender. Keep the oven on after you have removed the potato.

If you do not have time you can cook the potato in the microwave. To do this leave the potato unpeeled and pierce the skin 5-6 times, place in a microwaveable bowl, cover with a small plate, and microwave for 5-7 minutes, rotating halfway through.

Around 10 minutes before the potato is due to come out of the oven (or while it is in the microwave), place the drained and rinsed beans in a saucepan of boiling hot water and cook on high for 8-10 minutes in order to soften them.

In a large bowl combine the potato and beans, and use a potato masher or a large fork to mash them both together. Add the onions, tahini, vinegar, garlic powder, cajun spice, salt, pepper, and flour and continue to mash until the mixture has thickened and all ingredients are well combined.

The oven should be preheated to 400° / 200°. Grease a baking tray with some oil.

Equally divide potato mixture into 8 patties, shaping and flattening them into a round burger shape then place on the greased baking tray. Bake for 10-15 minutes, carefully turning each burger half way through with a spatula.

A few minutes before the burgers are due to come out of the oven lightly toast the buns and prepare the smashed avocado by placing the flesh in a bowl with lime and chili and cruising with a fork.

Serve burgers straight from the oven while warm crisp and golden. Garnish with smashed avocado, tomato, and lettuce.

They will store for 1-2 days in the fridge or 4 weeks in the freezer.

REFRIED BEAN & ROASTED SWEET POTATO QUESADILLAS

This easy and delicious meatless meal combines mashed sweet potatoes with hearty and filling refried beans for a satisfying and crowd-pleasing meal. You could also serve this with a side of Vegan Sour Cream to add a creamy element.

Preparation Time
10 minutes

Total Time
1 hour
(including cooking
time for sweet
potato)

Makes
2 as a main or 4 as
a side dish

INGREDIENTS

2 medium sweet potatoes, peeled & sliced
4 tbsp olive oil, divided
2 tsp cumin powder
2 tsp paprika powder
½ tsp coarse salt
¼ tsp ground black pepper

4 white tortillas
2 cups refried beans
2 tbsp jalapenos, finely chopped
1 avocado, chopped

DIRECTIONS

Preheat the oven to 400° / 200°.

In a small bowl combine 2 tablespoons of oil, cumin, paprika, salt, and pepper. Place the sweet potatoes in a baking dish and pour the oil spice mixture over, coating all sides of the potato.

Bake in the oven for 40 minutes or until the potatoes are cooked throughout and slightly caramelised on the edges.

Heat a large frying pan with oil over medium heat. Place the tortilla on the plate and spread with ¼ of the sweet potato mix, ¼ of the refried beans and a few chunks of avocado over half of the tortilla wrap, then fold it over. Carefully transfer it to the frying pan using either a spatula or by very carefully sliding the tortilla from the plate onto the pan. Press down using the spatula and cook for 2-3 minutes on each side.

Remove from the heat and transfer to a serving plate.

Repeat with remaining wraps and filling and serve while hot and crispy.

BEAN TOSTADAS WITH PICO DE GALLO

Flavorsome little tostadas are piled high with homemade refried beans and topped with fresh and authentic pico de gallo, avocado, and cilantro. This super easy and healthy meal is sure to become a weeknight staple.

Preparation Time
20 minutes

Total Time
40 minutes

Makes
4 servings

INGREDIENTS

8 mini corn tortillas

FOR THE REFRIED BLACK BEANS:

1 tbsp olive oil
1 heaped tsp cumin seeds
½ medium onion, finely chopped
2 cloves garlic, crushed
¼-½ tsp cayenne pepper
½ tsp chipotle powder (optional)
2 cans (15oz / 425g) black beans
½ cup water
½ tsp salt

FOR THE PICO DE GALLO:

1 small red onion, finely chopped
4 ripe red tomatoes, seeds removed and diced
½ jalapeno, finely chopped (seeds removed depending on heat preference)
½ cup cilantro, roughly chopped
3 tbsp freshly squeezed lime juice

TO SERVE:

Lettuce, sliced
1 avocado, sliced
3 heaped tbsp cilantro

DIRECTIONS

Heat the oil in a skillet and once hot roast the cumin seeds for a minute until they start to change color and become fragrant. Stir in the onions and sauté for 5 minutes until they have softened.

Add the garlic, cayenne, and chipotle and cook for a minute. Next add the drained and rinsed beans, water, and salt and bring to a boil. Reduce to a simmer and cook for 10 minutes then remove from the heat and completely mash the beans using a potato masher or a fork, adding a tablespoon of water if the mixture is too dry.

Preheat the oven to 400° and line a baking tray with parchment paper.

Brush a little olive oil on both sides of the corn tortillas, or spray with cooking spray and bake for 7-10 minutes or until golden brown, turning once after 4 minutes to evenly cook on both sides.

Combine all ingredients for the Pico De Gallo in a medium bowl.

Once the tortillas have finished baking spread a few tablespoons of refried beans onto each one. Top with the pico de gallo, lettuce, avocado, and cilantro.

Serve immediately while the tortillas are warm and crisp.

MEXICAN POTATO SKINS WITH SOUR CASHEW CREAM

It's hard to believe this irresistible meal is actually healthy! Deliciously crisp potatoes skins are baked twice then filled with a smokey Mexican refried bean filling, and finally topped with raw vegan 'sour cream', avocado, scallions, and cilantro.

Preparation Time
10 minutes
(+ overnight to soak the cashew nuts)

Total Time
40 minutes

Makes
12 skins / 4 servings

INGREDIENTS

FOR THE SOUR CASHEW CREAM:

1 cup raw cashews, soaked in water overnight
1 tsp apple cider vinegar
1 tsp lemon juice
⅛ tsp salt

FOR THE POTATO SKINS & FILLING:

6 large potatoes, washed
2 tbsp olive oil, divided
1 small onion, finely chopped
2 large garlic clove, finely chopped
1 red bell pepper, chopped

½ tsp salt
2 tsp ground cumin
1 tsp smoked paprika
½ tsp chipotle powder (optional)
½ tsp cayenne pepper
2 cans (14.8oz / 420g) black beans
⅓ cup vegetable stock
1 small jalapeno, chopped
Juice of 1 lime
1 avocado, sliced
2-3 scallions, sliced
A handful of chopped fresh cilantro

DIRECTIONS

FOR THE SOUR CASHEW CREAM

Drain and rinse the cashew nuts and place them in a food processor or blender with the apple cider vinegar, lemon, and salt. Blend until completely smooth, scraping down the sides a few times with a spatula. Add 1 tsp water at a time if the cashew sour cream is too thick.

Transfer the cream to a bowl, cover with cling film and chill in the fridge while you make the potato skins.

FOR THE POTATO SKINS:

Preheat the oven to 375°. Line a baking tray with parchment paper.

Place potatoes in a saucepan and cover with enough water to fully submerge them, then bring the water to a boil. Boil for 3 minutes then remove from the heat, drain the water and run cold water over the potatoes to stop them from cooking and to cool them down.

Cut the potatoes in half, lengthwise and use a melon baller or teaspoon to carefully remove the potato flesh, leaving ⅛" of potato flesh to hold the filling.

Brush the potato skins with 1 tbsp olive oil and sprinkle with a little salt then bake in the oven for 15 minutes. Increase the heat to 420° and continue to bake for 10 minutes until the potato edges have browned.

While the skins are in the oven you can move onto the filling. Heat 1 tbsp oil in a frying pan and sauté onions for 3-4 minutes until soft. Add garlic and spices for 1-2 minutes until fragrant then stir in the red pepper and salt, cooking for 5 minutes until it has started to soften. Add a drizzle of water if the mixture appears to be too dry.

Add the black beans with the vegetable stock and cook for

10 minutes until most of the water has evaporated. Mash half of the black beans with a potato masher or fork then add the jalapeno and lime and give everything a good mix.

Remove the potatoes from the oven and the black beans from the stove. Fill each potato skin with beans, a dollop of cashew cream, a slice of avocado and a sprinkle of scallions, and cilantro leaves.

Serve immediately.

CHEESY AVOCADO ENCHILADAS

These mouthwatering vegan black bean & avocado enchiladas are stuffed with fresh ingredients and smothered in a homemade enchilada sauce for an authentic Mexican experience, any night of the week.

Preparation Time
15 minutes

Total Time
45 minutes

Makes
6 enchiladas

INGREDIENTS

2 tbsp olive or vegetable oil
2 medium garlic cloves, finely chopped
1 white onion, sliced
1 red bell pepper, sliced
1 (15oz / 420g) can black beans
1 (15oz / 420g) can chickpeas
2 large avocados, chopped
1/3 cup nutritional yeast
3 medium tomatoes, chopped
2 tsp cumin powder
1 tsp paprika
1/2 tsp cayenne pepper
1/2 tsp salt
1/4 tsp pepper
6 large tortillas

FOR THE ENCHILADA SAUCE:

2 tbsp olive or vegetable oil
3 cups vegetable stock
1/2 cup tomato puree
1/4 cup all-purpose flour
2 tbsp olive oil
2 tsp cumin powder
1/2 tsp chili powder
1/4 tsp garlic powder
1/4 tsp onion powder
1/2 tsp dried oregano
1 tsp sugar
1/2 tsp coarse salt
1/2 tsp freshly ground black pepper

DIRECTIONS

Heat a large frying pan with oil over medium heat. Once hot add onions and peppers and saute for 4-5 minutes until soft.

Add garlic and fry for 1-2 minutes.

Reduce heat to low and add cumin, paprika, and cayenne, stirring constantly for 30 seconds until the spices are fragrant.

Add the chopped tomatoes, avocado, nutritional yeast, black beans and chickpeas, and mix well. Heat for 5-6 minutes then remove from the heat and set aside.

Next prepare the enchilada sauce. In a small bowl combine flour, cumin, chili, garlic, onion, oregano.

Heat a saucepan with oil over medium heat. Once hot add the tomato paste and fry, moving it around frequently for 30 seconds. Slowly add the flour and spice mixture and mix well to combine. Cook for 30 seconds to 1 minute using a whisk to stir constantly.

Pour in the vegetable stock and sugar and bring mixture to a boil, then reduce heat and simmer for 8-10 minutes until the sauce has thickened and reduced.

Preheat the oven to 350° / 175° and grease a 9x13 inch oven dish with a little oil.

Place tortilla wraps on a clean surface and evenly distribute the bean mixture between the 6 wraps, rolling each one tightly and tuck in the ends, then transfer to the greased oven dish.

Pour over the enchilada sauce, covering each wrap and bake for 25 minutes.

Serve immediately while hot.

ONE-POT MEXICAN QUINOA

Easy to make, versatile and extremely flavorsome, this Mexican spiced quinoa is a fail-proof recipe which will compliment most main meals perfectly. Try serving it with a salad or refried beans.

Preparation Time
10 minute

Total Time
35 minutes

Makes
4 servings

INGREDIENTS

1 tbsp olive oil
2 cloves garlic, finely chopped
1 jalapeno, finely chopped
1 cup uncooked quinoa
1 cup vegetable stock
1 (15oz / 420g) can kidney beans
1 (15oz / 420g) can chopped tomatoes
1 cup corn kernels, fresh or

frozen
1 tsp chili powder
1 tsp cumin powder
1 tsp paprika
½ tsp coarse salt
½ tsp ground black pepper
1 avocado, chopped
1 lime, freshly juiced
2 tbsp fresh cilantro, chopped

DIRECTIONS

Heat olive oil in a large saucepan or pot over medium heat. Once hot add the garlic and jalapenos and cook, stirring frequently, for 1 minute. Add chili powder, cumin, and paprika and stir frequently for 30 seconds.

Stir in quinoa, vegetable stock, beans, chopped tomato, corn, and seasoning and bring to a boil.

Reduce heat to low, cover the pot, and simmer for 20 minutes.

Remove from heat, uncover and stir in avocado, lime juice, and chopped cilantro.

Transfer to a serving bowl and serve immediately.

CRISPY BAKED TOFU FAJITAS

The word "Fajita" derives from the Spanish word "Faja," meaning strip. In this recipe you'll use strips of beautifully flavored tofu and bake them in a sticky Mexican glaze before wrapping them in tortillas along with fresh veggies.

Preparation Time
10 minutes
(+ 20 minutes
to press and
marinade the tofu)

Total Time
40 minutes

Makes
4 servings

INGREDIENTS

1 lb / 450g extra-firm tofu
½ cup light soy sauce
4 tbsp vegetable oil, divided
1 tbsp brown sugar or maple syrup
2 tbsp nutritional yeast (optional)
½ -1 tsp cayenne pepper
1 tsp cumin powder
1 tsp dried oregano

2 tbsp oil
1 small carrot, thinly sliced
1 red bell pepper, thinly sliced,
1 portobello mushroom, thinly sliced
2 tbsp fresh cilantro, roughly chopped
4 large tortilla wraps

DIRECTIONS

To start, remove tofu from packaging and press between two towels to remove excess water. You can use something weighted, such as a large saucepan or a heavy chopping board and place this on top of the tofu to squeeze out as much moisture as possible for a minimum of 10 minutes. This process will allow the tofu to absorb much more flavor. After 10 minutes slice the tofu into long thin strips.

In a medium bowl combine soy sauce, maple syrup or sugar,

nutritional yeast, cayenne pepper, cumin, oregano and 2 tbsp oil. Add the tofu, coating well, and leave to marinade for a minimum of 10 minutes (you can prepare this the night before and leave it in an airtight container in the fridge for optimal flavor).

Preheat the oven to 350° / 170°. Line a baking tray with parchment paper.

Place the tofu on the baking tray in a single layer and pour what is left of the marinade sauce over the tofu.

Bake for 30 minutes, turning twice.

10 minutes before the tofu is due to finish cooking heat a frying pan over medium-high heat with 2 tbsp oil and saute the vegetables for 8-10 minutes. Remove tofu from the oven and and it to the vegetables along with cilantro, cook for a minute.

Place the tortillas in a warm oven or heat in the microwave for 30 seconds to 1 minute until soft and warm.

Place ¼ of the tofu filling in a tortilla and wrap tightly. Continue with remaining filling and wraps. Serve immediately while hot.

CHILI CON VEGGIE

This brilliant alternative to the classic chili con carne is rich, hearty and meat-free. It's packed full of pulses, high in fibre and has a welcoming kick of chili!

Preparation Time
10 minutes

Total Time
1 hour 10 minutes

Makes
4 servings

INGREDIENTS

1 tbsp olive oil
1 large onion, finely chopped
2 garlic cloves, finely chopped
1 fresh red chili
1 tbsp cumin powder
1 tbsp ground coriander
1 tbsp paprika
½ - 1 tsp cayenne powder
1 tbsp dried oregano
½ tbsp dried parsley
1 medium carrot, finely chopped
1 heaped tbsp tomato purée
1 can (15oz / 420g) red kidney beans
1 can (15oz / 420g) pinto or navy beans
1 can (15oz / 420g) chopped tomatoes
2 ½ cups / 600ml vegetable stock
8.5oz / 250g dried red split lentils
1 tsp coarse salt
¾ tsp freshly ground black pepper
2 tbsp fresh cilantro, roughly chopped

DIRECTIONS

Heat olive oil in a large pot over medium heat. Once hot add onions and saute for 3-4 minutes then add garlic, chili, cumin, coriander powder, paprika, cayenne, oregano, and parsley and fry for a minute.

Add the carrot, mixing well and pour in the two cans of drained and rinsed beans. Crush a few of the beans using a fork or a wooden spoon. This will give the chili a thicker and creamier texture.

Add the tomato puree and stir constantly for 30 seconds then add the lentils and pour in the chopped tomato and stock. Bring to a boil then reduce to a low simmer and cook for 1 hour, stirring occasionally.

Remove from the heat, season, then stir in chopped cilantro and serve over rice or inside a tortilla wrap.

QUINOA STUFFED PEPPERS

Serve these vibrant stuffed peppers on any occasion, from a busy weeknight to guests at a dinner party - you can even keep the leftovers for lunch the following day! Not only are they quick to make but they are also jam packed with fresh veggies.

Preparation Time
10 minutes

Total Time
20 minutes

Makes
4-6 servings

INGREDIENTS

½ cup quinoa, uncooked
1 cups vegetable stock
½ can (approx 7oz / 200g) black beans
½ medium carrot, grated
1 celery stalks, finely chopped
¼ medium onion, finely diced
2 cloves garlic, minced
¼ cup peas, fresh or frozen
¼ cup corn, fresh or frozen

½ tsp onion powder
½ tsp garlic powder
½ tsp coarse salt
½ tsp ground pepper
½ tsp cayenne pepper
½ tsp cumin powder
½ cup tomato sauce

4 large bell peppers, any color

DIRECTIONS

Preheat the oven to 350° / 170. Line a small ovenproof dish (5x10-inch) with baking paper and set aside.

Bring 2 cups of vegetable stock to a boil then add quinoa. Stir, then cover and cook for around 15 minutes. Once cooked drain any excess water and set aside.

In a large saucepan mix beans, grated carrot, celery, onions, garlic, peas, corn, and all spices together and heat for around 7 minutes over medium-low heat.

Add cooked quinoa and tomato sauce, mixing well, and heat for 5 minutes.

While the vegetable mixture is cooked you can prepare the peppers.

Cut the top off each bell pepper and place in the ovenproof dish. Stuff each pepper with the quinoa mixture and transfer to the oven.

Bake for 30-35 minutes until the pepper has softened and the top has browned.

WHITE BEAN & AVOCADO BURRITOS

This easy, filling and delicious dish is sure to become one of your go-to weeknight meals. The burritos are baked in the oven, making this tasty Mexican meal super healthy.

Preparation Time
25 minutes

Total Time
50 minites

Makes
4 servings

INGREDIENTS

FOR THE RICE:

1 cups brown rice
1 cup vegetable stock
1 cup water

FOR THE FILLING:

½ cup vegetable stock
3 cloves garlic, finely chopped
1 medium onions, chopped
1 ½ tsp cumin powder
3 cups mushrooms, chopped (any variety)
2 bell peppers, sliced (any color)
1 jalapeno peppers, finely chopped
1 tbsp fresh cilantro, chopped
1 ½ cups white beans (Butter beans, Cannellini beans etc)
¼ cup tomato sauce

2 tbsp nutritional yeast (optional but recommended)
½ tsp coarse salt
½ tsp freshly ground black pepper
¾ cup corn, fresh or frozen

FOR THE TOMATO SAUCE:

1 cup plain tomato sauce
1 tsp garlic powder
1 tsp onion powder
2 tsp granulated sugar
2 tbsp fresh cilantro, chopped
1 tsp cumin

FOR THE BURRITOS:

2 large avocados, peeled pitted and chopped
8 large tortilla wraps

DIRECTIONS

Preheat the oven to 350° / 175°. Grease one or two large

casserole dish (around 9x13-inch).

TO MAKE THE RICE:

Pour water and vegetable stock into a saucepan and bring to a boil. Add rice, cover and simmer for 15-17 minutes until cooked. Set aside.

TO MAKE THE BURRITO FILLING:

Heat 1 tbsp vegetable oil in a large pot over medium-high heat and saute the onions for 3-4 minutes until soft. Add the garlic and cumin and cook for a minute.

Pour in a splash of the vegetable broth and add the mushrooms, peppers and jalapenos, frying for 3-4 minutes until the vegetables have softened.

Pour in the remaining vegetable stock along with the white beans, cilantro, tomato sauce, nutritional yeast and seasoning. Heat the mixture for 4-5 minutes.

Remove from the heat and very carefully transfer 1/3 of the burrito filling into a blender or food processor and blend until smooth. Add it back into the pot of beans and stir in corn. Set aside.

TO MAKE THE TOMATO SAUCE:

In a medium bowl mix together tomato sauce, garlic powder, onion powder, sugar, cilantro and cumin.

TO ASSEMBLE THE BURRITOS:

Lay the tortilla wrap on a clean surface such as a chopping board or large plate.

Fill with just under ½ cup of burrito filling, ¼ cup rice a few tbsp of tomato sauce and a small handful of avocado. Wrap tightly and tuck in the ends.

Continue with remaining filling and wraps. Place each burrito seam side down and bake in the oven for 25 minutes.

There may be some leftover rice and burrito filling which will keep well for up for 4 days in an airtight container in the fridge.

.

FAJITA PASTA

This recipe is super easy - you simply throw all of the ingredients into a big pot and leave it to allow the flavors to marry together while the pasta is cooking. Clean up is easy too as you need just one pot to cook the entire meal!

Preparation Time
10 minutes

Total Time
20 minutes

Makes
4-6 servings

INGREDIENTS

1 lb / 450g pasta
1 (15oz / 420g) can chopped tomatoes
1 ½ cup vegetable stock
2 cups water
2 tbsp chili sauce
1 red onion, thinly sliced
4 large cloves garlic, finely chopped
2 bell peppers, thinly sliced
1 tsp dried chili flakes

1 tsp coarse salt
1 tbsp cumin
2 tsp smoked paprika
¾ tsp cayenne powder
1 tsp dried oregano
2 tbsp fresh cilantro, plus extra for garnish
2 tbsp olive oil
½ tsp freshly ground pepper
1 lime, cut into wedges

DIRECTIONS

In a large pot add dry pasta, tomatoes, vegetable stock, water, chili sauce, onion, garlic, peppers, dried chili flakes, cumin, paprika, cayenne powder, cilantro, oil, and pepper.

Bring mixture to a boil and cook for 10-12 minutes until the sauce has thickened and reduced, stirring frequently.

Serve immediately and garnish with lime wedges and chopped cilantro.

SIDES

MEXICAN GAZPACHO

This refreshing chilled soup is perfect for a warm summer's evening or served at a BBQ. It packs a healthy punch, filled with ingredients like tomato, peppers and cucumber.

Preparation Time
5 minutes

Total Time
10 minutes

Makes
4 servings

INGREDIENTS

1 ¼ cups cucumber, chopped and peeled, divided
½ cup red or green bell pepper, chopped
2 tbsp red onion, finely chopped
1 tbsp jalapeño pepper, finely chopped
1 tbsp white vinegar

½ tsp sugar
¼ tsp coarse salt
½ tsp dried oregano
¼ - ½ tsp tabasco or other hot sauce
1 garlic clove, chopped
1 (15oz / 420g) can chopped tomatoes
¾ cup water

DIRECTIONS

Place 1 cup of cucumber, pepper, red onion, jalapeño pepper, white vinegar, sugar, salt, dried oregano, tabasco sauce and garlic in a food processor and pulse until well combined and broken down but not completely smooth. If you prefer your gazpacho completely smooth feel free to blend for longer.

Remove from the food processor and pour into a large bowl. Stir in water and chopped tomatoes. Cover with cling film and chill in the fridge for a minimum of 2 hours, preferably overnight.

When you are ready to serve, divide the soup into 4 bowls and top each bowl with 1 tablespoon of chopped cucumber.

CALABACITAS CON ELOTE (ZUCCHINI WITH CORN)

A very popular side dish commonly served as street food in Mexico. This colorful dish is fresh, healthy and 100% vegan! Perfect served in a warm tortilla wrap or over brown rice.

Preparation Time	**Total Time**	**Makes**
10 minutes	30 minutes	4 servings

INGREDIENTS

1 tbsp olive oil
1 red onion, peeled & chopped
3 cloves garlic, finely chopped
¼ tsp ground cumin
2 plum tomatoes, chopped

2 large zucchini, diced
1 fresh poblano chili or jalapeno pepper, chopped
1 cup frozen corn kernels
1 (15oz / 425g) can black beans
½ tsp salt

DIRECTIONS

In a large skillet heat olive oil over medium heat. Once hot sauté onions for 3-4 minutes then add garlic, stirring for a minute. Add cumin, tomatoes, zucchini, chili, corn, beans, and salt. Stir well, cover, and cook for 10-12 minutes until the zucchini has softened and the corn has thawed.

When you remove the lid some liquid may have gathered at the bottom of the pan. If this is the case cook the mixture over a higher heat for another few minutes until all the liquid has evaporated.

Transfer to a serving dish and serve immediately while hot in a tortilla wrap or as a side dish.

Calabacitas is great served cold and will keep in an airtight container in the fridge for up to 3 days.

CORIANDER LIME RICE

A delicious dish that can be eaten alone or as the perfect accompaniment to a main dish. The fresh lime and cilantro really bring this meal to life and transforms plain rice into something very special.

Preparation Time	Total Time	Makes
5 minutes	20 minutes	4 servings

INGREDIENTS

1 cup uncooked dry rice
(long grain is the best to use)
2 cups water + ½ tsp salt
1 large lime, zested and juiced
½ cup fresh cilantro, chopped
1 tsp coarse salt

DIRECTIONS

Place 2 cups of water and salt in a saucepan and bring to a boil. Stir in rice and cover. Reduce the heat to low and simmer for 15-17 minutes without removing the lid.

Add lime juice, zest, cilantro and salt, and mix well to combine.

Transfer to a serving plate and serve immediately while hot.

CLASSIC GUACAMOLE

A classic dish that requires no introduction. This tried and tested recipe is simple, quick and incredibly tasty. You can keep it smooth or chunky, and if you don't plan to serve it immediately just leave the avocado pit in the guacamole bowl and cover with plastic wrap to prevent any browning.

Preparation Time
5 minutes

Total Time
5 minutes

Makes
4-6 servings

INGREDIENTS

4 ripe avocados, chopped
2 tbsp lime juice, freshly squeezed
1 medium ripe tomato, seeded & chopped
1 jalapeno, finely chopped
1 garlic clove, finely chopped
½ small red onion, finely chopped
½ cup fresh cilantro leaves, chopped
½ tsp coarse salt
¼ tsp freshly ground black pepper

DIRECTIONS

Lightly mash the avocado in a medium bowl then add remaining ingredients, mixing well but gently to avoid crushing the avocado too much. You want to keep it chunky so that it retains a nice texture.

If you're not serving it straight away, place a stone in the guacamole (this helps to stop it going brown), cover with plastic film and chill until needed.

EASY REFRIED BEANS

'Frijoles Refritos' is a traditional staple dish in Mexico and consists of cooked beans that have been authentically spiced and then mashed, transforming a rather boring side dish to a flavor-packed feature!

Preparation Time
10 minutes

Total Time
20 minutes

Makes
4-6 servings

INGREDIENTS

1 medium white onion, finely chop half and leave the other half whole
½ tsp cumin powder
½ - 1 tsp chili powder
2 (2 x 15oz / 420g) cans pinto or black beans
1 cup vegetable stock

2 sprigs fresh oregano or 1 tsp dried oregano
2 medium garlic cloves, unpeeled
¾ tsp coarse salt
6 tbsp vegetable oil

DIRECTIONS

Heat a large frying pan with vegetable oil and once hot add the chopped onion, cooking over medium heat for 5-6 minutes until soft. Add the cumin and chili powder and stir constantly for 30 seconds.

Pour in the drained and rinsed beans and mix well, cooking over low heat for 2 minutes, then add 1 cup of stock and the fresh oregano. Bring to a boil then reduce to a low simmer for 10 minutes. Using a potato masher or the back of a wooden spoon mash the beans until a chunky 'puree' has formed. You can mash according to your preference.

Season with salt and pepper then cook the refried beans for 2-3 minutes until desired consistency is reached. If they appear to be drying out simply add a splash or water or stock, one tablespoon at a time.

CHILAQUILES WITH LENTILS

Chilaquiles is a Mexican breakfast or side dish that features fried crispy tortilla chips tossed with a rich and spicy tomato sauce and traditionally served with a fried egg on top. This easy vegan version is healthy and nutritious and will keep you energized all morning.

Preparation Time
10 minutes
(+ 20 mins to
rehydrate the chili)

Total Time
30 minutes

Makes
2 servings

INGREDIENTS

FOR THE RED SAUCE

4 large ripe tomatoes
2 large cloves garlic, finely chopped
½ onion, cut into quarters
1 large guajillo or ancho chili
½ tsp ground cumin
¼ tsp salt
¼ tsp sugar

FOR THE CHILAQUILES

1 tsp olive oil
1 small red onion, finely chopped
4 cloves garlic, finely chopped
1 jalapeno, chopped

1 tsp ground cumin
1 tsp sweet paprika
½ tsp smoked paprika
1 tsp oregano
¼ tsp cinnamon
⅓ cup corn kernels, fresh or frozen
1 (15oz / 425g) can brown lentils
¼ tsp or more salt

2 corn tortillas or 1 ½ cups tortilla chips
½ lime
¼ cup fresh cilantro, chopped

DIRECTIONS

Place the dried chili in 1 cup of hot water for 20 minutes to rehydrate. Drain the chiles, reserving the water it was soaking in.

Preheat your broiler.

Line a baking tray with foil and place the tomato, garlic, onion, and chili on to it. Grill the vegetables for 5-10 minutes, turning once or twice to ensure all sides are evenly cooked. Cook until charred on the outside. Remove and place in a food processor along with half a cup of water that the chili was soaked in, cumin, salt and sugar and blend until you have a smooth sauce. Set aside.

To make the filling heat olive oil in a skillet and once hot sauté the onions for 5 minutes until soft. Fry the garlic and all of the spices for a minute then add the corn, lentils, and seasoning. Cover and cook for 10 minutes, adding a dash of water if the filling gets too dry. Remove from the heat.

If you are using a tortilla wrap you will need to bake these at 350° for 5-7 minutes in order to get them crispy then remove from the oven and roughly chop them into 'chips'. Fold in tortilla chips with a spatula.

Serve immediately while hot with the red sauce spooned over the filling. Garnish with cilantro and a squeeze of lime juice.

KALE & SPINACH SALAD WITH CREAMY AVOCADO DRESSING

This salad is a slightly altered version of a traditional Mexican street salad which combines super healthy kale and spinach with beans and corn, all tossed in a sensationally flavorsome creamy avocado dressing.

Preparation Time
5 minutes

Total Time
5 minutes

Makes
6 servings

INGREDIENTS

FOR THE SALAD:

2 packed cups kale, stalks removed & chopped
2 packed cups spinach, chopped
1 (15oz / 420g) can kidney beans
¾ cup corn, fresh or frozen
1 red bell peppers, finely chopped
1 large avocado, finely chopped
1 ripe tomato, finely chopped

2-3 scallions, finely chopped
½ cup cilantro, finely chopped
1 tbsp jalapeños, seeded & minced

FOR THE DRESSING:

½ large avocado
½ cup warm water
½ lime, freshly squeezed
1 tsp cumin
¾ tsp salt
½ tsp ground black pepper

DIRECTIONS

Combine all salad ingredients in a large bowl. Set aside.

Add all dressing ingredients to a food processor or blender and pulse until smooth.

If you plan to consume the salad in one day then pour the dressing over the salad, mixing well. However, if you think you will have leftovers it is better to add dressing just before you are serving as it will make the salad slightly soggy and brown. To keep, refrigerate the salad and dressing separately for 24 hours

7 LAYER MEXICAN DIP

This recipe combines other side dishes from this cookbook and layers them all together to create a delicious, exciting and surprisingly healthy dip. If each element is readily available the recipe takes no time, however, if you need to prepare each layer it will take longer - but will certainly be worth it!

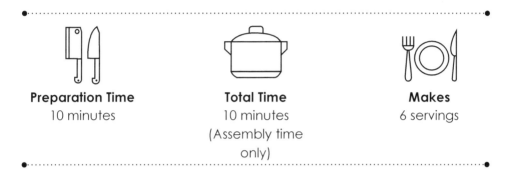

Preparation Time
10 minutes

Total Time
10 minutes
(Assembly time
only)

Makes
6 servings

INGREDIENTS

2 cups refried beans, store bought or homemade
¾ cup vegan Mexican 'Queso'
1 cup guacamole, store-bought or homemade
1 cup salsa, store bought or homemade

½ bell pepper, thinly sliced
1 handful black olives, chopped
1 handful fresh cilantro, chopped
Large bag of tortilla chips, for serving

DIRECTIONS

To Assemble the Dip:

Take a large bowl and spread the refried beans on the bottom, smoothing the top with the back of a spoon. Next spread the guacamole, and then a layer of salsa. Top with queso cheese, a layer of red peppers and finally sprinkle olives and cilantro on top.

Serve immediately with tortilla chips or cover tightly with cling film and store in the fridge for 1 day.

VEGAN ELOTE (MEXICAN STREET CORN)

This popular Mexican street food is easy to replicate at home for an authentic flavor of South America. The corn is slathered in a delicious creamy chili and lime sauce and then grilled to perfection.

Preparation Time
10 minutes
(+ 4 hours for cashews to soak)

Total Time
20 minutes

Makes
4 servings

INGREDIENTS

4 corn cobs, husks removed
1 cup raw cashew nuts
½ cup water
½ tbsp apple cider vinegar
½ tsp dried chili flakes
½ tsp cayenne powder
½ tsp cumin powder
½ tsp paprika

½ tsp turmeric powder
1 garlic clove, finely chopped
Juice of one lime, freshly squeezed
2 tbsp fresh cilantro, roughly chopped
Olive oil, for greasing baking tray

DIRECTIONS

Place cashew nuts in a small bowl and top with water, vinegar, lime juice, chili flakes, cayenne, cumin, paprika, turmeric and garlic. Give it a good stir and allow the nuts to soak for at least 1 hour, or preferably up to 4.

Pour cashew nuts and liquid into a blender and pulse until fully combined.

Preheat the grill to high heat and line a baking tray with foil. Drizzle a little olive oil on the baking tray.

Bring a saucepan of water to a rolling boil and carefully drop in corn, boiling for 3 minutes.

Remove the corn and discard the water. Pat the corn dry with a kitchen towel to remove as much water as possible.

Transfer corn to the baking tray and coat evenly with the cashew mixture.

Grill corn for 10-15 minutes, turning once or twice.

Remove from grill and garnish with cilantro.

EXTRAS

ROASTED GARLIC MASHED POTATOES

These fluffy, warm and crisp Mexican rolls are most commonly eaten by cutting one end off, scooping out the insides and stuffing it with a filling of your choice - such as refried beans, salsa or chili.

Preparation Time
40 minutes

Total Time
2 hours 50 minutes
(incl. time for the
dough to rise)

Makes
12 rolls

INGREDIENTS

2 ¼ tsp or 1 package active dry yeast
2 cups warm water (between 105° - 115°)
1 tsp sugar
4 – 4 ½ cups bread flour
1 tsp coarse salt

1 tsp vegetable shortening
Good quality olive oil for greasing

DIRECTIONS

Place the yeast and sugar in a small mixing bowl and stir in the water. Leave for 5 minutes for the mixture to froth and bubble. If it does not then your yeast is inactive and you will need to start again.

Break the shortening into small pieces and add it to the yeast mixture, along with salt and 3 cups of flour. Mix on low using a stand mixer fitted with a dough attachment or using your hands. If the dough appears a little too sticky add a tablespoon of flour at a time in order for it to come together.

Knead by hand or using your stand mixer on low for around 10 minutes. The dough needs to be soft, smooth, and elastic. It should ping back when you lightly press a finger into it.

Lightly grease a large bowl with a little olive oil and place the dough inside, turning it over to coat all sides. Cover with a damp kitchen towel and leave undisturbed in a warm place for 1 - 1 ½ hours or until the dough has doubled in size.

Grease a baking sheet with a little olive oil and set aside.

Place the dough on a clean lightly floured surface and knead for 1-2 minutes, then roll into a log and using a knife divide into 12 even pieces. Roll each piece between your palms and make an oval shape, tapering the ends a little.

Transfer each roll onto the greased baking tray, ensuring both sides are coated with oil. Repeat with remaining dough then place a slightly damp kitchen towel on top and set aside for 40 minutes in a warm place for them to rise again.

After 40 minutes, preheat the oven to 370° / 190°. The rolls should have doubled in size again.

Score each roll a few times using a sharp knife, starting at the tapered side and working your way down in horizontal swipes.

Gently brush each roll with a little more olive oil then bake in the preheated oven for 27-30 minutes until golden brown.

Remove from the oven and cool for a few minutes on a wire rack.

Serve immediately while warm and crusty or leave to cool for later.

They will keep at room temperature in an airtight container for up to 3 days, and you can reheat them in the oven at 370° / 190° for 2-3 minutes.

HOMEMADE TACO SAUCE

With only 5 minutes preparation time, there would be no reason not to make your own sauce rather than use store bought. The combination of spices gives this sauce an authentic flavor that you won't find in a jar. The sauce freezes well so you could make extra to ensure you always have some to hand.

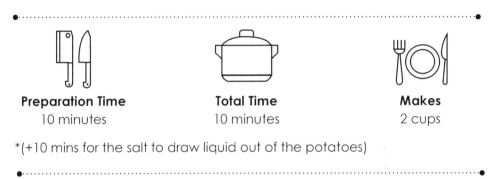

Preparation Time
10 minutes

Total Time
10 minutes

Makes
2 cups

*(+10 mins for the salt to draw liquid out of the potatoes)

INGREDIENTS

2 cups tomato puree
1 tbsp cumin powder
1 tbsp hot or smoked paprika
½ tsp onion powder
1 tsp garlic powder
1 tsp dried oregano
⅛ tsp coarse salt
⅛ tsp ground black pepper
⅓ cup water
1 tsp white wine vinegar
1 tsp maple syrup
¼ to 1 tsp dried chili flakes
¼ to 1 tsp cayenne pepper

DIRECTIONS

Place all ingredients into a small saucepan and bring to a boil over medium heat. Reduce to low and simmer for 10 minutes in order for the sauce to thicken. If you prefer a thicker sauce leave it to simmer for 15 minutes.

Remove from the heat and cool to room temperature.

The sauce will keep for up to 5 days in an airtight container in the fridge.

VEGAN SOUR CREAM

This quick and easy vegan sour cream is as close to the real thing as you can get! It is wonderfully rich and creamy, with a lovely flavor and perfect amount of 'tang'. Use it as a non-dairy alternative for dips and toppings.

Preparation Time
15 minutes
(+ overnight to
soak cashews)

Total Time
35 minutes

Makes
1 cup

INGREDIENTS

1 cup raw unsalted cashew
nuts (soaked overnight)
1 tbsp apple cider vinegar
Juice of 1 lemon
⅛ - ¼ tsp coarse salt
½ tsp nutritional yeast
⅓ - ½ cup water

DIRECTIONS

Drain cashews and place in a blender with vinegar, juice from ½ the lemon, salt and start with ⅓ cup of water. Blend until very smooth, adding more water as required, depending on how thick you would like the sour cream. Taste for lemon and add more if required.

Store in an airtight container in the fridge for up to 1 week.

CHIMICHURRI SAUCE

This popular piquant South American sauce differs according to which region it hails from. The Mexican version features a punchy flavorsome combination of herbs, garlic and lemon, amongst many other mouthwatering ingredients. It goes perfectly with almost anything- try it with tofu, drizzled over vegetables or even as a dipping sauce.

Preparation Time	**Total Time**	**Makes**
5 minutes	5 minutes	1 ½ - 2 cups

INGREDIENTS

1 cup olive or vegetable oil
¼ cup lemon juice, freshly squeezed
½ cup flat-leaf parsley, finely chopped
¼ cup cilantro leaves, finely chopped
2 tbsp garlic, finely chopped

1 tbsp red onion, finely chopped
1 tbsp dry oregano
1 tbsp chili flakes
1 tsp coarse salt
½ tsp black pepper

DIRECTIONS

Combine all ingredients in a large mixing bowl. Cover with cling film and chill in the fridge for a minimum of 2 hours before serving for the flavors to marry.

Keep in an airtight container in the fridge for up to 2 weeks.

RESTAURANT STYLE SALSA

This tried and tested recipe for salsa is made in a food processor with tomatoes, cilantro, and jalapenos. The perfect combination of ingredients provides a fresh, tangy and chunky salsa that's sure to be a real crowd pleaser.

Preparation Time
5 minutes
(+ 30 minutes to
chill)

Total Time
10 minutes

Makes
4 cups

INGREDIENTS

2 (15oz / 420g) cans chopped tomatoes
3 cloves garlic, peeled
2 small fresh green chiles
1 bunch (about 2 cups loosely packed) fresh cilantro
½ large white onion, finely chopped
1 jalapeno, stem removed

1 tsp ground cumin
1 tsp coarse salt
1 tsp sugar
2 tbsp freshly squeezed lemon or lime juice
2 sprigs fresh oregano or 1 tsp dried oregano
¼ tsp ground black pepper

DIRECTIONS

Drain the can of chopped tomatoes if you prefer a thicker salas.

Place all ingredients in a food processor and pulse until you have reached your desired consistency. Taste to check if more salt or pepper is needed.

Chill, covered, for a minimum of 30 minutes for the flavors to marry.

Salas will keep for 3-4 days in an airtight container in the fridge.

SALSA VERDE

Salsa Verde is traditionally made with parsley, but this version features cilantro, jalapenos and lime juice for a punchy Mexican alternative.

Preparation Time
5 minutes

Total Time
10 minutes

Makes
2 cups

INGREDIENTS

1 tbsp olive oil
1.4lbs / 650g tomatillos (green tomatoes), husks removed, roughly chopped
1 large jalapeno pepper
¼ medium onion
2 garlic cloves

½ cup cilantro leaves, chopped
1 tbsp lime juice
1 ½ tsp red wine vinegar
1 tsp dried oregano
½ tbsp coarse salt

DIRECTIONS

Heat olive oil in a large pan over medium-high heat. Add tomatillos, onions and jalapeno and saute for 3-4 minutes until slightly caramelised.

Remove from the heat and carefully transfer into a blender. Add garlic, cilantro, lime juice, red wine vinegar, oregano and salt, and pulse until combined.

Transfer to an airtight container and refrigerate for 6-7 days.

VEGAN MEXICAN CHEESE

Here you have the only vegan cheese recipe you'll ever need to satisfy any cravings. Whether you want to sprinkle some cheese flavoring onto a fajita or burrito, spread some onto bread or use a queso to pour over nachos, this simple easy and delicious cheese can seriously rival any dairy based version.

Preparation Time	Total Time	Makes
10 minutes	10 minutes	1-2 cups

INGREDIENTS

SHAKEABLE CHEESE:

1 cup raw cashews
3 ¼ tbsp nutritional yeast
¾ tsp coarse salt
¼ tsp ground black pepper
½ tsp cumin
¼ tsp cayenne powder
½ tsp garlic powder
¼ tsp onion powder
¼ tsp paprika

SPREADABLE CHEESE:

1 ½ cups raw cashews
3 tbsp nutritional yeast

½ tsp coarse salt
¼ tsp garlic powder
½ tsp cumin
¼ tsp cayenne pepper
1-2 tbsp olive oil

QUESO:

1 cup of the spreadable cheese
Up to ½ cup of hot water

DIRECTIONS

FOR THE SHAKEABLE CHEESE:

Add all ingredients to a food processor and pulse in short bursts until a fine powder forms. You do not want to pulse for long periods at a time to prevent a puree from forming. Store in an airtight container in the fridge for up to 6 days and use to sprinkle on burritos, fajitas, tacos etc.

FOR THE SPREADABLE CHEESE:

Place the cashew nuts in a food processor and pulse until completely broken down until a smooth paste is formed. Scrape down the sides as you go along to ensure all of the nuts are incorporated. Add the cumin, garlic powder, cayenne, nutritional yeast and seasoning. Pulse until fully combined. Add one tablespoon of olive oil and blend for 1-2 minutes to form a spread. Adding a second spoon of oil will produce a much thinner spread.

Store in an airtight container in the fridge for up to 6 days.

FOR THE QUESO:

Make the spreadable cheese and place desired portion into a medium bowl. Very slowly add hot water and continue to whisk after each addition to make a pourable cheese.

This cheese is perfect as a dip or to pour on top of nachos.

Store in an airtight container in the fridge for up to 6 days.

DESERTS

HORCHATA (SWEET MEXICAN RICE MILK)

This cinnamon-vanilla frothy drink is a Mexican favorite, consisting of a milky, creamy yet dairy-free drink that has been thickened using rice milk. Perfect as a refreshing drink in the summer or heated up for a comforting warming drink when it's cold.

Preparation Time
50 minutes

Total Time
10 minutes

Makes
4 cups

*(+ overnight for the rice to soak and 2-3 hours for Horchata to chill)

INGREDIENTS

1 cup basmati rice
4 cups water
1 cinnamon stick
1 tbsp maple syrup
1 tsp cinnamon powder
½ tsp vanilla extract

DIRECTIONS

Place the rice and cinnamon stick in a glass bowl or large glass container and leave to soak overnight.

The following day, pour the entire contents - rice, water and cinnamon stick into a blender and add the vanilla and maple syrup. Blend until everything is pulsed and there are no large pieces left.

Pour the mixture through a sieve with a bowl underneath and discard the rice/cinnamon pieces.

Cover the bowl with cling film and chill in the fridge for 2-3 hours.

Serve in a glass over ice and add a pinch of cinnamon.

MEXICAN HOT CHOCOLATE

This wonderfully rich and creamy hot chocolate is spiced up with a pinch of cayenne pepper, and, of course, is 100% vegan. The flavor is also enhanced with cinnamon and nutmeg, making this the perfect warming drink for a cold winter's night. You could also spike it by adding a glug of Tequila!

Preparation Time
5 minutes

Total Time
10 minutes

Makes
2 servings

INGREDIENTS

2 cups dairy-free milk
3 ½ tbsp cocoa powder
2-3 tbsp maple syrup
½ tsp ground cinnamon
¼ tsp nutmeg
¼-⅛ tsp cayenne
1 tsp vanilla extract
⅛ tsp coarse salt

DIRECTIONS

Pour milk into a small saucepan and bring to a gentle simmer over low heat.

Add cocoa powder, cinnamon, nutmeg, cayenne, vanilla, maple syrup, and salt and whisk constantly for a minute until all ingredients are fully combined.

Pour into heatproof glasses or mugs and serve immediately with an extra sprinkle of cinnamon on top of each mug.

CRISPY MEXICAN CHURROS

Churros are long, fluted cinnamon donuts that are crispy on the outside and moist and fluffy on the inside. They are a truly decadent delight, which can be devoured plain or dipped in vegan chocolate sauce.

Preparation Time
5 minutes

Total Time
15 minutes

Makes
4 servings

INGREDIENTS

1 cup water
2 ½ tbsp white sugar
½ tsp coarse salt
2 tbsp vegetable oil
1 cup all-purpose flour
3-5 cups oil for frying
½ cup white sugar, for dusting
1 tsp ground cinnamon
Pastry bag, for piping

DIRECTIONS

Combine water, 2 ½ tablespoons sugar, salt, and 2 tablespoons oil in a small saucepan and bring to a boil. Once boiling remove from heat.

Slowly stir in flour until mixture becomes a dough.

Heat the oil in a large pan over medium-high heat to 190°.

Once hot place dough in a pastry bag and pipe strips into the hot dough. Fry the dough in batches depending how big your pan is. You do not want to overcrowd the pan.

Fry churros for 3-5 minutes until golden and crisp. Once cooked, remove each churros using a slotted spoon and transfer to a paper towel lined plate.

Once all churros are cooked combine sugar and cinnamon in a separate bowl and sprinkle onto, ensuring all sides are well coated.

Serve immediately while hot and crispy.

PINEAPPLE & APPLE EMPANADAS

Common in the South American region, Empanadas usually consist of pastry filled with a savory filling and baked until golden brown and crispy. This unique take on a traditional dish features a sweet pastry that is filled with spiced apples and pineapples, making a special dessert or sweet treat.

Preparation Time
15 minutes

Total Time
40 minutes
(+ 15 minutes for
the dough to chill

Makes
12 empanadas

INGREDIENTS

FOR THE EMPANADAS:

2 cups all purpose flour, sieved
1 ½ tbsp raw or caster sugar
1 tsp salt
1 tsp baking powder
⅓ cup vegan butter or vegetable shortening, cut into small cubes
½ cup cold water
2 tbsp dairy free milk, for the glaze

FOR THE FILLING:

1 large apple, peeled and finely chopped
1 cup pineapple chunks (fresh or canned), finely chopped
½ tbsp maple syrup
¼ tsp cinnamon powder
⅛ tsp nutmeg powder

DIRECTIONS

In a large mixing bowl combine flour, sugar, salt, and baking powder.

Add the butter then rub the butter and flour in between your fingertips until it has all been incorporated and the mixture resembles breadcrumbs.

Slowly add the water with a wooden spoon until a dough has formed then gently knead it until it comes together. Cover with plastic wrap and chill in the fridge for 15 minutes.

While the dough is in the fridge you can prepare the filling by combining all filling ingredients together in a bowl and mixing well. Set aside.

Preheat the oven to 350°. Line a baking tray with parchment paper.

Lightly flour a clean work surface and roll the dough out. Cut 12 circles of about 3 ½ -inches in diameter. Pour the dairy-free milk into a small bowl.

Place 2 tablespoons of the filling in the center of each circle. Dip your finger in the dairy free milk and trace around the outer edge to help the pastry seal. Fold the circle of pastry in half to create a half circle and seal the edges by gently pressing down with a fork.

Brush the pastry with a little soy milk and score a few holes using a fork or a sharp knife to allow steam to escape.

Transfer the empanadas to the baking tray and bake for 15-20 minutes or until golden brown.

Leave the empanadas to cool for 10 minutes before serving as the filling will be piping hot.

.

CHILI CHOCOLATE AVOCADO MOUSSE

This chocolate avocado mousse is creamy and decadent, with a hint of chili to add a real Mexican kick. You'll be surprised to know this dessert is actually healthy as it is full of antioxidants and nutrients from the cacao powder and avocado - and best of all it takes just 5 minutes to prepare.

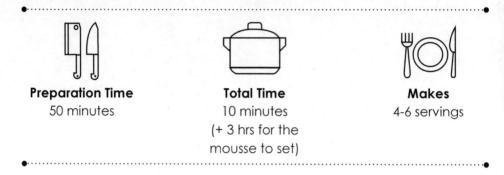

Preparation Time
50 minutes

Total Time
10 minutes
(+ 3 hrs for the mousse to set)

Makes
4-6 servings

INGREDIENTS

2 ripe avocados
½ cup raw cacao powder
½ cup full-fat coconut milk
¼ cup maple syrup
2 tsp vanilla extract
⅛ tsp coarse salt
⅛ - ¼ small red chili
1 ½ tsp cinnamon, divided

DIRECTIONS

Place all ingredients, except ½ tsp cinnamon, into a food processor and blend until completely smooth.

Taste to check if you wish to add more maple syrup or chili.

Spoon mousse into serving bowls and dust each bowl with a pinch of cinnamon.

Cover with cling film and leave to set in the fridge for a minimum of 3 hours.

MAYAN SPICED CHOCOLATE PUDDING

This vegan version of a Mayan dessert is thick, rich, and indulgent and features traditional spices such as cinnamon, allspice, and chili powder. A wonderfully decadent dessert that is simple and easy to make. You can sub cayenne for ancho chili powder if you are unable to source it.

Preparation Time
10 minutes
(+ 4 hours for the
puddings to chill)

Total Time
10 minutes

Makes
4 servings

INGREDIENTS

1 (14oz / 400g) can coconut milk, divided
¼ cup cornstarch
¼ cup sugar
¼ tsp ground cinnamon
⅛ tsp ground allspice
¼ tsp ancho chili powder

⅛ tsp salt
½ tsp fresh orange zest
3oz / 85g vegan dark chocolate, finely chopped
1 tsp vanilla extract

DIRECTIONS

Prepare 4 small ramekins.

In a medium mixing bowl combine ¼ cup of coconut milk with the cornstarch and whisk well until no lumps remain. Set aside.

In a medium saucepan add the remaining can of coconut milk, sugar, cinnamon, allspice, chili powder, salt, and orange zest. Bring to a gentle simmer then add the cornstarch mixture.

Stir continuously for 2-3 minutes until the mixture has thickened and reduced. Remove from the heat and add the chocolate and vanilla, stirring constantly until the chocolate has melted.

If you find after a minute that there are still some large chunks of chocolate, place it back on a very low heat for 30 seconds then remove from the heat and stir again. You want to avoid burning the chocolate as unfortunately this will ruin the entire pudding.

Transfer the chocolate pudding into the prepared ramekins, allow to cool to room temperature, sprinkle with a little chili powder, cover with plastic wrap and chill in the fridge for a minimum of 4 hours or overnight.

BUÑUELOS (CINNAMON-SUGAR CRISPS)

These light, crispy and sweet strips are sprinkled with cinnamon sugar and make a wonderful after dinner treat. They keep well in an airtight container and are great to have on hand to satisfy a sweet tooth.

Preparation Time
5 minutes

Total Time
30 minutes

Makes
50 to 60 strips

INGREDIENTS

1 cup white caster sugar
1 ½ tsp ground cinnamon
¼ tsp ground nutmeg
1 tsp vanilla powder
(optional)
12 eight-inch plain tortillas
Vegetable oil (for frying)

DIRECTIONS

In a large freezer bag or a deep, shallow dish combine sugar, cinnamon and nutmeg. Set aside.

Cut the tortillas into strips of around 3x2 inches.

Heat 1 inch of oil in a heavy bottomed pan. Heat the oil until it reaches 190°. If you do not have a thermometer, test the oil with a piece of tortilla, which should sizzle when it touches the oil and should brown in about 2 to 3 minutes

Fry the tortillas in batches, making sure to not crowd the pan as this will prevent the Buñuelos from getting crispy. Once golden brown and crisp, remove the strips with a slotted spoon and transfer to a paper towel lined plate for a few seconds to remove some excess oil.

While hot place in the sugar-cinnamon mixture, making sure to mix well and fully coat.

The Buñuelos will keep for 3-4 days in an airtight container at room temperature.

MORE GREAT TITLES

• •

HIGH CEDAR PRESS

CHECK OUT THE FULL COLLECTION!

70262964R00053

Made in the USA
San Bernardino, CA
27 February 2018